# How to Ruin Your Financial Life

# Other Hay House Titles by Ben Stein

*How to Ruin Your Life*
(also available as an audiocassette and CD)

*How to Ruin Your Love Life*

*Yes, You Can Be a Successful Income Investor!*
by Ben Stein and Phil DeMuth (available October 2004)

## $ $ $

# Hay House Titles of Related Interest

*The Abundance Book,* by John Randolph Price

*Attitude Is Everything for Success,* by Keith D. Harrell

*Feng Shui DOs & TABOOs for Financial Succe$$,*
by Angi Ma Wong

*How to Make One Hell of a Profit and Still Get to Heaven,*
by Dr. John F. Demartini

*Money Cards,* by Suze Orman

*Suze Orman's Ultimate Protection Portfolio*

*10 Secrets for Success and Inner Peace,*
by Dr. Wayne W. Dyer

*The Trick to Money Is Having Some!,* by Stuart Wilde

## $ $ $

All of the above are available at your local bookstore,
or may be ordered by visiting:
Hay House USA: **www.hayhouse.com**
Hay House Australia: **www.hayhouse.com.au**
Hay House UK: **www.hayhouse.co.uk**
Hay House South Africa: **orders@psdprom.co.za**

# How to Ruin Your Financial Life

## Ben Stein

**HAY HOUSE, INC.**
Carlsbad, California
London • Sydney • Johannesburg
Vancouver • Hong Kong

**Published and distributed in the United States by:** Hay House, Inc., P.O. Box 5100, Carlsbad, CA 92018-5100 • *Phone:* (760) 431-7695 or (800) 654-5126 • *Fax:* (760) 431-6948 or (800) 650-5115 • www.hayhouse.com • *Published and distributed in Australia by:* Hay House Australia, Ltd., 18/36 Ralph St., Alexandria NSW 2015 • *Phone:* 612-9669-4299 • *Fax:* 612-9669-4144 • www.hayhouse.com.au • *Published and distributed in the United Kingdom by:* Hay House UK, Ltd. • Unit 62, Canalot Studios • 222 Kensal Rd., London W10 5BN • *Phone:* 44-20-8962-1230 • *Fax:* 44-20-8962-1239 • www.hayhouse.co.uk • *Published and distributed in the Republic of South Africa by:* Hay House SA (Pty), Ltd., P.O. Box 990, Witkoppen 2068 • *Phone/Fax:* 2711-7012233 • orders@psdprom.co.za • *Distributed in Canada by:* Raincoast • 9050 Shaughnessy St., Vancouver, B.C. V6P 6E5 • *Phone:* (604) 323-7100 • *Fax:* (604) 323-2600

*Editorial supervision:* Jill Kramer    *Design:* Summer McStravick

**Library of Congress Cataloging-in-Publication Data**

Stein, Benjamin, 1944-
  How to ruin your financial life / Ben Stein.
     p. cm.
  ISBN 1-4019-0241-3 (Hardcover)
  1. Finance, Personal. I. Title.
HG179.S824 2004
332.024—dc22

                                        2003018587


                                ISBN 1-4019-0241-3


                        07  06  05  04    4  3  2  1
                           1st printing, March 2004


                    Printed in the United States of America

$ $ $

*For my wonderful friends*
*Barron and Steve.*

$ $ $

# CONTENTS

# $ $ $

# Introduction

# $ $ $

"The world rests on three pillars: on money, on money, and on money." So goes an ancient East European proverb. We can also look around the world to China and one of their Confucian axioms: "No money, no life."

Then again, we can look even closer and recall the words of the immortal Bob Dylan. About ten years after he burst riotously onto the cultural scene, an interviewer asked him why his lyrics weren't as angry as they had been when he started out in Greenwich Village.

"It's hard to be bitter when you're as rich as I am," said the Bobster (or words to that effect).

But we really don't have to look to great poets or ancient proverbs for financial wisdom. Money is simply a great thing to have. It may not be able to buy happiness, but it sure gives a good impression of a long-term lease. In fact, now that I think about it, maybe money *can't* buy happiness, but money comes as close to the ability to buy happiness as anything outside yourself can.

Let me count just a few of the ways: With money, you have financial and material security—

which is a giant part of life, especially when you don't have any. The fear of financial insecurity is one of the most lethal destroyers of human happiness, a creator of anxiety and paranoia, and a wrecker of a decent night's sleep. When you have money, you don't have these problems, at least not nearly as much. Money also allows for a high degree of freedom and choice—such as the ability to travel at will, the choice of living in magnificent mansions, of driving sleek cars, of consorting with fast women and sultry men, of enrolling your sullen children in the best private schools, of purchasing magnificent art for your walls and tables, and of buying fashionable clothes and sparkling jewelry that make your friends green with envy.

With money you can give gifts to charities, build shelters for animals, send food to the starving, erect dwellings for the homeless, and give money to your relatives. In other words, with money . . . you can not only do well, but do good.

Without money, you go to bed worrying about how to pay your MasterCard bill. You can't help anyone, not even yourself. Appeals from perfectly good causes go unanswered. However, with money, you can go to sleep thinking about what you want to buy the next morning, and who you can help out. This, as you can see, is a very good thing.

With money in your pockets and in your stock brokerage account, you can go into any store or car dealership or travel agency with your head held high. The map of the world is not a fantasy or a dream or an abstraction. It's your travel itinerary any old time you feel like going—and going first class, of course—not in coach with an obese stranger sitting on your lap and a stale bag of peanuts thrown at you by a surly flight attendant. Money is fresh salmon and caviar at 40,000 feet eaten off china on top of a linen placemat, with a hot fudge sundae for dessert.

Having money cannot automatically cure disease, but it can sure buy you better doctors and far, far better care than you'd get with a penny-pinching HMO. It can allow you to buy the best medicines, get them refilled as often as you want, make sure your physician sees you first, and give you the option to take the kind of long rests the doctor orders. Plus, it can ensure the type of serenity and peace of mind that builds a far healthier immune system.

Money cannot buy love . . . well, just forget that one. Money *can* buy love—it's time to put that old lie to rest. Men and women *do* love other men and women who have money. It makes the homely seem better looking, the fat seem less corpulent, and the weak and sickly seem more robust. Money confers an aura of beauty around the otherwise not-so-beautiful. And, yes, money can make men and women fall in love with you and stick to you like glue. Maybe this isn't the way life *should* be, but this is the way it is.

Perhaps, most important of all, money buys respect. A man may be of middling intellect, slow in his speech, doddering in his gait, and not at all witty, but if the people around him know that he has tons of cash, he garners respect. And the more money he has, the more respect he gets. It's quite a phenomenon to sit at Morton's or Le Cirque and witness waiters, busboys, and wine stewards—not to mention lawyers, film studio heads, and movie stars—fall all over themselves before billionaires. Perfectly respectable *millionaires* actually tug at their forelocks in the presence of billionaires and cringe as if they were coal miners in 19th-century England meeting the local Earl of whatever.

"Nobility is riches sanctified by long passage of time," goes the English saying. Here in America, nobility is just plain having money. We don't have dukes or earls or viscounts here. We do have immense respect for money, though, and the words "He's rich" or "She's a billionaire's daughter" are the equivalent of saying, "He's a prince" or "She's a duchess."

But you don't have to be a billionaire to reap the joys of having money. In *David Copperfield,* Charles Dickens wrote: "Annual income twenty pounds, annual expenditure nineteen nineteen six, result happiness. Annual income twenty pounds, annual expenditure twenty pounds ought six, result misery."

The main thing is to have enough money to live comfortably, with some reasonable degree of security, with the ability to enjoy the good things in life that definitely *do* come with money.

You don't have to race a Donzi speedboat or fly a Gulfstream jet, and you don't have to own racehorses in order to experience the joy and security that money can bring you. But you do have to have enough cash to feel secure at night if your boss starts picking on you and you realize you may soon be looking for a new job. You need to have enough moolah to make sure that your spouse and children can see the very best doctors if they get sick. Basically, you just have to have enough of it so that you know you're well protected. A life lived in or on the edge of deprivation is simply not the same as one that's lived in comfort. One is enjoyment—the other is just eking out an existence.

Yet, despite the clear desirability of having money, millions of people don't have the funds they need and want. This, alas, is the case despite the fact that there are thousands—maybe tens of thousands—of books out there telling people how to make, save, spend, and invest money wisely. (How well I know—I've written a few of them.) They make some impact, but the vast numbers of people in this country (and others) simply don't get it when they're advised how to handle money and how to manage their financial lives. (I didn't get it the first few hundred times myself.) They just keep on doing the same messy things that got them into trouble in the first place.

So in light of the above, I decided that it was time for a different approach. I thought I'd offer some pertinent advice in reverse . . . by creating a book that tells you, the reader, how to *ruin* your financial life. By doing so, I figured I'd allow you to see just what you're doing wrong, and how *what* you're doing wrong fits into a recognizable pattern of ruination. (By the way, it's a pattern I've seen in those close to me—in fact, under my own skin on many a day.)

If, as you're reading this book, you see that you're doing 75 percent of the things that people do to wreck their financial lives, then maybe you'll wake up and realize that your financial mess didn't happen by chance. It happened because you were doing certain clear, specific things wrong that get everyone who does them into hot water. If you realize that your actions and inactions will inevitably lead to grief, maybe you'll stop doing those things . . . and start to pull your financial life together. In any event, that was the hope with which this book was written. We Americans, British, Canadians, Australians, New Zealanders, Israelis, free people, create our own financial reality.

$ $ $

Now, what qualified me to write this little tome? First, I've been following money and its uses and misuses all my life, and by now I'm 58, so I've been doing this a long time. I've made a large number of the mistakes in this book—not just once or twice, but many times. The results have been predictably calamitous. When I stopped doing those harmful things, the results were predictably good.

Second, I had a father who was a highly insightful guy when it came to money. He never made a truly huge income, although it was certainly not a small income, but he always had money and lived in comfort, and he was able to leave my sister and me a meaningful sum. And I observed how he did it. To be truthful, I haven't always done as well as he did, but if your father is a wizard, you do grow up learning *some* magic.

Third, I'm fascinated by how some people have money and comfort, and how others have neither, and I've long been a manic observer and classifier of how success and failure come to pass. I'm bound to say that I've learned more from the failures than from the successes, and I think you will as well. (Maybe some bit of levity will help, too.) In every action I take, I try to ask myself, "Am I behaving like so-and-so who went into bankruptcy?" or "Am I behaving like my dad, who had a gift for avoiding the pitfalls that leave men and women in desperation?"

Or, to put it another way, when I was a child, we lived in a neighborhood with people who had fancier cars than we did, played at elegant country clubs, and thought nothing of laying down a handful of bills on a horse. They all wound up broke. I try not to do anything in the way that they did. I have friends here in Hollywood who made excellent incomes for decades and now can't afford to take a vacation. I try to avoid doing what they did and do, too. Instead, I try to put myself in the mold of the people who wake up each day knowing that they can pay their bills not just for this day, but for a decade, without worrying too much about where the next dollar is going to come from.

Years ago when I told my father that I could

buy a certain estate (which was bigger than I really needed) and still be years away from being in the neighborhood of poverty, he said, "Good, because that's a neighborhood you never want to be in." That's what this book is about. Do the things in this book consistently, and you'll find yourself in the neighborhood of poverty. Do them very rarely, and you'll sleep soundly at night in a nice neighborhood.

Let me make this point as clear as possible: This book is called *How to Ruin Your Financial Life* for a reason: If you follow the rules in it, you *will* ruin your financial life. If you do the opposite, sunny days lie ahead.

Without further ado, here are the 55 rules. I'm positive that I've probably missed some ways in which you can ruin your financial life— maybe even some important ones—but let's just get on with it. My motto, borrowed from the genius editor Jim Bellows, applies here in spades: "Begin at once, and do the best you can."

# How to Ruin Your Financial Life

# 1

## $ $ $

## Forget about Tomorrow

How many of you remember that great old 1950s song called "Forget Domani"? It basically advised the listener to forget about "tomorrow" (*domani* in Italian) and just live for today.

Well, that's what you should do, too—forget about tomorrow. That's right. It's always today. Tomorrow will never come at all, so don't make any plans for the future. Making plans is a lot of work, and thinking about the future is frightening. It's a lot easier to just think about today.

Plans for the future involve calculations and variables and may require some form of self-discipline—yuck. Plus, there's so much uncertainty about the future that sometimes you don't really feel good when you think about it. So why think about it at all? It's just a way to get prematurely gray. Instead, think about what fun you can have now, and how much enjoyment and spending you can cram into one day.

And do not make any financial plans—oh no. Forget about making any deposits to a savings account or an Individual Retirement Account (IRA) or a Keogh. Those things are for people who worry about money and end up making themselves sick.

I mean, come on, tomorrow will be just like today. You have enough to eat today, right? You have enough to wear, you own a car, and you have a roof over your head, don't you? Well, then, you'll always be so fortunate because that's just the way things tend to work out in your life.

There's a famous weather-forecasting rule that says that 60 percent of the time the weather tomorrow will be like the weather today. And that's how it will be in your financial life. That means: Don't worry yourself about it. And, oh, that other 40 percent? That will be even *better* than the weather today. Which brings us to the next rule . . .

# 2

## $ $ $

### Know with Certainty That There Will Never Be Any Rainy Days in Your Life

There's a lot of talk among old people about saving for a rainy day. You may even have parents or grandparents who lived through the Great Depression of the 1930s or the terrible recession and inflation of the 1970s. They may tell you that things won't always be great economically. There could be a recession, or a new inflation or deflation, or a real-estate collapse, they'll say. You could lose your job. It happened to them, after all. That's why, they'll tell you, you need to put aside money for "a rainy day."

The only problem with this admonition is that it doesn't apply to you. There will be no rainy days in *your* life. Whatever you have now in terms of work, housing, and savings, you will always have. Those bad old days of economic uncertainty are long, long gone. Now we live in a sunny haze of certainty and security. The government's brilliant financial analysts have learned to manage the national economy so that there can never be another really bad economic downturn.

Or, if there is one, it will only last a few days.

On a more personal level, it's just a waste of your good time to consider the possibility of a recession or layoffs at work. These things will simply never happen, and if you plan for them, then you will have penalized yourself by saving money, and not splurging on that vacation or new car you wanted.

Just go on with your life knowing that all is fundamentally well, and that the bad things that happened to other people in other eras will simply never happen to you. It's that basic. You don't need to make any plans for economic security because your life will never have any downs, only ups.

And anyway . . .

# 3

## $ $ $

### Remember That Your Peace of Mind Is a Lot More Important Than the Few Pennies You'll Save Worrying about Money

Let's face it. It's a bit upsetting to think about money. It involves mathematics, and maybe you were never very good at math. It involves discussions of the future, and as we've already come to realize, those discussions can be supremely boring and frightening . . . plus, they're irrelevant to you because it's already been decided that your future is going to be just like your past, only better. When you think about money and the months and years ahead, you have to ponder such things as growing older and the possibility of not having a job—

and these are definitely distressing thoughts.

Not only that, but if you start thinking about the future and your financial situation, you might come to the realization that you'll have to make some changes in your life. This might require some self-denial. That's a lot like dieting or exercise—only worse. And that makes it painful to think about.

So, do yourself a favor. Just don't think about saving money—or planning for the future—at all. Go on with your daily routine of life, happy as a clam, content with what you're doing, and don't change a thing. You're calm right now, so why disturb the peace by torturing yourself with worries and plans and financial portfolios and savings accounts? Simply put all that out of your mind.

# 4

## $ $ $

## Save Money Only When You Feel Like It, and If You Just Don't Feel Like Saving, Then Don't!

After all, what is saving? It's taking money from present consumption and putting it in a dark vault where you don't have access to it and can't spend it at will. But think about it: What's the good of money if it's hidden away like that? It will just get cold and lonely. But in *your* hands, if you can spend it on something you really enjoy, that money is hard at work making you happy. Sure, you could put the money in a savings account or a CD and it might show up every month as a typed entry on a piece of paper, but what fun is that? It's way better to spend, spend, spend and live it up—and maybe meet a cute guy or gal in the process.

You *could* invest your money in a stock-market account, but then every month you'd get a statement that's complicated and hard to understand. Some months it would show that you were up, and some months you'd be down. (And what a drag it would be to open up that envelope and see you've lost some of your hard-earned cash! You're better off not having that account at all!)

But if you buy several new cashmere sweaters or a new set of golf clubs, you can use and enjoy them right now. And you'll never open a monthly statement that says your Fair Isle sweaters and Big Bertha clubs have gone down the tubes!

Besides, saving is such an abstract concept that involves all kinds of vague notions about uncertainty and the future. Whereas a trip to the Bahamas is real and warm and sunny—and will give you memories for a lifetime.

So spend as much as you can, right here and now. Live for the moment!

# 5

## $$$

## Don't Bother to Learn Anything at All about Investing

Life is short—far too short to spend your free time reading some dusty old tome on investing your money. Who does that kind of thing anyway? Nerds and worrywarts, and goofy guys with Coke-bottle glasses and pens in their pockets. You're *far* too cool to even think of poring over books with charts and graphs and explanations of why stocks are sometimes better than bonds, and bonds are sometimes better than stocks. Who needs that kind of stuff? Not a hotshot party animal like you who can stay up till 3 A.M. drinking vodka martinis and still be at work at 8! Not someone who has the youth and vitality and smarts that you do.

Leave all that reading and researching

nonsense to cranky old folks who have nothing better to do with their time. As for you, you have to get down and get funky. You have to know about J. Lo's latest movies and whether her latest romance with Ben Affleck is working out. These are the things that count in your life.

Plus, you have fascinating TV shows to watch, stomach crunches to do so you can stay in shape, and important phone calls to make to your buddies from college. I mean, what's important? *The National Enquirer* and the latest scoop on what really happened on *The Bachelor,* or devastatingly dull statistics on interest rates?

I think you know the answer to that one.

# 6

## $ $ $

### Spend As Much As You Want, and Don't Be Afraid to Go into Debt

What does that mean? It means that in *your* case, and only in your case, you need not pay any heed to balancing income and outgo. Or, in other words, spend as much as you feel like spending and don't worry about it.

For most people and most situations, there has to be some sort of cause and effect. Or so the old folks say. If you eat a lot, you get fat. If you eat a little, you get thin. If you spend more than you earn, eventually you go broke. If you spend less than you earn, you can and do save. If you save a lot, eventually you get rich.

These seem like simple truths. But maybe

they're just a bit *too* simple. Do those supposed "truths" take into account that you look really great in that hand-tooled leather jacket? Or that if you buy that new car you'll be the envy of everyone at work? Do those rules take into account that you're a living, breathing guy or gal with blood and heart and desires? Heck, no!

If you see something for sale that you want and need (like that 50-inch plasma TV), you have to buy it whether it puts you into the red or not. After all, life is short and you have to enjoy every minute of it.

Now, what about those people who would try to rain on your parade and say, "Hey, you can't just get further and further into debt"? Well, what about them? Isn't the federal government chronically in debt? It seems to just stay that way year after year, yet no one thinks the federal government is going anywhere. Anyway, there are always people sending you letters offering to lend you money, right? There are always new credit cards arriving in the mail. So what's the problem?

Why do you have to be any different from our esteemed government? If they want a new highway or a new aircraft carrier, they get it, right? Well, *you* want a new bracelet and a trip to Vegas. Maybe both you and the government have to go into debt over it, but so what? Just go for it right here and now, and damn the debt! Win the war to be hip, and then worry about your debts later. In fact, worry about them "tomorrow," because as we've already mentioned, tomorrow never comes!

# 7

## $ $ $

### Set Up a High-Profile, High-Consumption Lifestyle with Enormous Fixed Expenses That You Can't Afford

What is life all about? In a few words, looking good to yourself and to others. "To Look good" is probably as short and sweet a reason for why men and women were put on the planet as I've ever heard. I think it was a character in an F. Scott Fitzgerald story who said that the goal of life was to ". . . live fast, die young, and leave a good-looking corpse. . . ." Sounds logical to me. And if looking good is the best thing in life, "feeling good" might be a close second.

It looks good to have a great car. And it makes you happy. So what if the car costs a fortune, your monthly payments are outrageous, and you barely earn enough to pay your rent?! You have to look good no matter what you earn. In fact, you have to look even better if you *don't* earn a lot of money so that people around you will *think* you're doing well. That's where fancy cars, designer clothes, and Pilates all come into play. They make you look good, and that's what counts both on the inside and the outside. That matters a lot more than penny pinching. So what if buying that golf cart overdraws your checking account? It makes you look awfully sharp on the course—and you can always charge it and pay for it over many years—all for a trifling 18 percent interest.

Being cool really comes down to this: High school never ends. And who were the coolest kids in high school? The ones with the best toys. Now it's still high school, whether you're 25 or 55, and you're still really only making the scene if you have the hippest clothes, the newest car, and have just returned from the most elite vacation spot. And if some Scrooge-like accountant warns you that you're overdoing it, tell him to stuff it. After all, life is short. You have to go for it with all the gusto you can right now. Party hearty, dude!

And here's something else to think about: If there's one thing you can be certain of as your expenses mount, it's that one of the most enjoyable things in the whole world is to have a magnificent home. The feeling you get when you walk into a stately mansion or ocean-view condo is one of deep pride and inestimable joy. Plus, people drive by your home and envy you. They ooh and ahh—and isn't arousing the envy of other people one of the best ways to spend money—even if you can't afford to?! What better use is there for money than to make you feel like a big shot? And so what if it makes your friends secretly hate you? At least they're impressed, right? At least they're paying attention to you.

So go even further into debt to set up that high-profile, exorbitantly expensive lifestyle by purchasing the home of your dreams. But wait—there's more, as the TV pitchmen say! Once you've bought the house, don't just let it look like some college dorm room. No! Make sure it's furnished extravagantly. Hire a decorator. If possible, choose the same interior designer that some of the truly rich and famous people have used so that you can brag about *that,* too. To heck with the cost! Did Napoleon worry about the cost when he was building his palaces? Does Bill Gates worry about the cost of his lakefront house? No, and neither should you if you want to make the right impression.

Save money and live within your means? Ridiculous.

But impress your friends and make them seethe with jealousy over your opulent lifestyle? Priceless.

# 8

## $ $ $

## Compete with Your Friends to See Who Can Spend the Most

Perhaps I was too harsh in the preceding essay when I talked about arousing the envy and ire of your friends by flaunting that opulent lifestyle you can't really afford. Maybe, rather than doing that, you should set up a friendly little competition to see who can spend the most. For example, take your friends out to a really expensive restaurant and pick up the tab. Then dare your friends to take you to a comparable establishment and eat and repeat—that is, start the whole cycle again, all the while steadily increasing the amounts you're spending on yourself and them (the one with the most expensive lobster wins!).

Or maybe you should compete to see who can take the most expensive vacation. Or who can stay at the most elaborate and pricey hotels. If you really want to, you can set up a situation where you and your friends get sucked more and more into spending money you don't have—until you're all commiserating over your respective bankruptcies.

But don't worry about that now—it's fun to go for broke with your friends. The bigger the risk, the more fun you'll have!

# 9

## $ $ $

## Don't Balance Your Checkbook or Keep Track of What You Spend

Why should you? The bank will send you a little form if you're overdrawn, won't they? In the meantime, you'll want to avoid that uncomfortable feeling of being hemmed in by lots of numbers and columns of figures, and instead, just do what's fun and easy.

After all, you're not a machine. You can't be programmed to function like a human calculator. You need to be your own sweet, carefree self. Besides, if you keep track of how much you spend, it might depress you.

So please don't do it.

# 10

## $ $ $

### Forget to Pay Your Taxes

If you're self-employed, which many people are these days, then by all means do not pay your estimated quarterly taxes. It's a lot of bother to do all those computations, and even more of a drag to take money out of your account just to send it in to the government. Why does the government need the money anyway? They already have trillions. And they have legions of employees and office buildings, and lots of aircraft carriers and submarines. They do not need your few measly pennies. They don't care about you!

If the IRS does somehow track you down, demanding the money you owe them, then borrow a line from the immortal Steve Martin and say, "Hey, I forgot." What can they do? It's not like you're an ax murderer. You simply "forgot" (wink, wink) to pay your taxes. This is America, after all. What can they really do to you for not paying up? It's not like this is North Korea or Iran or something. This is a free country, and people are expected to cheat on their taxes—or not pay them at all if they don't want to. And really, who needs the cash more—you or Uncle Sam?

Now, here's another important point: If you have your taxes deducted from your paycheck every pay period, take the maximum number of deductions you can. Claim 12 exemptions even if you don't have any children. Then, when it comes close to April 15, just don't file your income taxes at all, period. That way you get to keep all of that extra money that wasn't withheld from your paycheck. It'll take years, maybe decades, for the IRS to catch up with you. And when they do, at most they'll just smack your hand and give you a big frown. They won't charge you immense interest and penalties. They won't seize your house and your boat and your car. They'll just say, "Well, pay when you can. We understand."

That's the IRS for you. The soul of compassion and forgiveness. Basically, this is an anti-tax country, from the President on down, so live that way and enjoy all that extra money that would have just been wasted by the government anyway.

Another great idea is to use tax shelters to avoid paying your taxes. That's right. Just by paying your accountant and/or your lawyer to draw up some papers and shifting some accounts around, the IRS will be completely fooled, and you won't have to pay a dime. And these things always work. Wait, what's that? You say you read in the newspaper about some tax shelters the IRS cracked down on and the courts invalidated? And you heard about people who had to pay back taxes in the hundreds of thousands and even millions? Well, that was them and this is you. *Your* tax shelters will be perfect and will hold water forever just because they're yours!

An added bonus: If you do get involved with litigating against the government over back taxes, you'll be amazed by how little tax lawyers charge. These attorneys will practically *give* away their services to you, and the fees and expenses will be comically low. And know that the IRS is not at all tenacious. Once they initiate a case, they'll ask you to pay your taxes a few times and then if you don't, they'll just give up and go on to the next guy.

Try it. You'll see. The IRS really just wants to be loved, same as you and me.

# 11

## $ $ $

## Truly Believe That You're Only As Valuable As What You Own

Look, this book is just between you and me, right? It's not as if anyone can read your mind and know what you're thinking. So, just between us, even though you're overweight, have a lousy job, and are miserable in your relationship, you know how to make yourself feel empowered, don't you? You know how to build your self-esteem. You know that the way to feel like a superhero is to buy the right things so you can feel great about yourself. You may be short and plump, but your sports car is always the right size. You might feel kind of threadbare on the inside of your soul, but your house is ornate—decorated with money you don't have.

You might be convinced that your friends are all secretly laughing at your failings (and maybe they are, tee-hee), but they won't laugh when they see you pull up in your ultra-cool new Jag sporting your new Rolex (that you charged at 12 percent interest). They'll think you're the last word in chic.

That's just how life goes, isn't it? I mean, no one really likes you—and you don't even like yourself that much—*if* you don't own the coolest stereo, the biggest flat-screen TV, and the most elegant luggage. This is a material world, and you—to coin a phrase—are a material girl . . . or guy. You can't expect to be liked for yourself—it's what you own that determines your self-worth . . . and your worth in the eyes of others.

So put yourself on that treadmill to oblivion. Spend and spend and spend . . . so you can own and own and own . . . and puff yourself up to the point where you finally feel proud of yourself.

You may have heard that happiness is an inside job. Baloney! Happiness comes from getting and spending. Happiness comes from piling up boxes and boxes of things you'll never use. Tommy Hilfiger, Von Dutch, Kate Spade, Armani, Gucci, Hermès, Mercedes-Benz, Ritz-Carlton—brands and labels are what matter, not self-esteem or a hard day's work or having loyal friends.

You're a nobody—in your own eyes and in the eyes of others—unless you buy and own every cool product and service out there . . . and don't you forget it.

# 12

## $ $ $

## Collect As Many Credit Cards As You Can, and Use Them Frequently

You're a citizen of an industrial first-world nation! You're a member of the ruling class. That means that you're entitled to have credit cards—lots of them. And why are credit cards named as such? Because, silly, they allow you to go on credit and buy things you otherwise couldn't afford!

Again, you're a 21st-century citizen! Credit is your right. More than that, going on credit is your civic *duty!* Yes, fellow citizen, what do you think would happen to this glorious nation if you stopped charging goods on your cards? It would be a disaster. Tens of millions of workers would be laid off. Corporate profits would vanish and the stock market would crash permanently. It would be as if a foreign invader had attacked and conquered this great land.

If you don't use your credit cards, you might as well be an agent of Al Qaeda. Well, maybe it's not that bad, but it's close.

So, don't be a saboteur of this nation we all love so much. Borrow, borrow, borrow, and spend, spend, spend. Remember that the credit card is your ticket to ride. It's your rocket ship to the moon. You're just not yourself without a wallet full of cards. You don't feel as if you have "The Power" without them—after all, doesn't some commercial tell you not to leave home without them? If you were limited to just spending what's in your pocket or in your checking account, you'd be cut off at the knees. And we don't want that to happen.

What is the one bold stroke through which you can help out the entire nation and at the same time make yourself feel empowered? Simple: Collect as many credit cards as you can, and max them out.

And then . . .

# 13

## $ $ $

## As Soon As You've Succeeded in Maxing Out Your Credit Cards . . . Get New Ones!

Credit-card application forms come in the mail every day. Make sure you fill out every one of them and acquire as many cards as you can. Don't even try to relate your income to your use of credit cards or your possession of them. Doing so would be madness. Don't try to make your life into a flow chart. I already told you, you're not a machine. Just get the cards and use them to buy what makes you feel good. This isn't just selfishness (as good as selfishness is), it's patriotism.

By the way, do you want to know a good test of whether or not you've overused your credit cards and are carrying too large a balance? Well, if the banks and credit-card companies are still offering you applications for cards, that shows that everything's fine and you have plenty of reserve spending capacity.

See, the credit-card companies have a super-computer buried in the Utah desert under thousands of feet of concrete. Its purpose is to take care of you and help you out. It monitors your credit-card use, and if it finds that you're using too much credit, it cuts you off in terms of new solicitations. This might seem like a rumor or an urban myth, but it's not. The fact is that the credit-card companies only want what's best for you—really. If they send you new credit cards, that means that you *need* new credit cards (as determined by that supercomputer) and that you can easily handle the load, so fill out those applications, mail them out, and watch the credit cards pour in.

And, closely related to this important directive is the following rule . . .

# 14

## $ $ $

### When You Get Your Credit-Card Bills, Pay Only the Minimum Each Month

You'll be pleasantly surprised to see just how little your minimum payment is when you get your credit-card statement each month. In fact, you can charge hundreds of dollars and the minimum will just be a paltry sum. You can charge *thousands* and your minimum might be as little as $100.

How can this be anything but great? I mean, why take on a burden you don't have to take on? And those late fees and finance charges—those items in small print that are listed at the bottom of your statement—well, what about 'em? Why should they get in the way of your having a good time? They'll never amount to much. So what if it takes you 20 years to pay off a $1,500 balance? As long as you're only making $20 payments each month, why bother thinking about how much the credit card company is making off you?

So, just pay the minimum and see how much your financial situation improves!

# 15

## $ $ $

### Know in Your Heart of Hearts That You Will Never Run Out of Money

You see, there *is* a good witch, like the one in *The Wizard of Oz*. The good witch makes sure that nothing bad will ever happen to you when it comes to money. This means that no matter how wildly you overspend, you'll never run out of cash. Never.

Well, maybe it's not a good witch, but it's somebody—maybe a father, a mother, a rich uncle, a fairy godfather—someone. And he or she is there to make sure you'll never have to file for bankruptcy or live on the streets.

So what if you can't readily identify someone in your family or social circle who will always bail you out or keep you from experiencing catastrophic financial losses? Don't worry about it. There *is* an invisible someone, somewhere who's looking out for you. You're immune from the fate that befalls those unfortunate others who lose their jobs, blow their trust funds, or bet the house on one hand in Vegas. You have that guardian angel. Those bad things can't happen to you. You're special. You'll always have plenty of moolah to spare. Plenty. And a good fairy sprinkling money all over you.

Count on it.

# 16

## $ $ $

### Repeat After Me: "I Am Not Responsible for My Financial Well-Being"

Well, why *should* you take on that responsibility? That would involve (again) a good deal of self-restraint, self-discipline, and abstinence when it comes to buying everything you've always wanted. If you *were* responsible for your own finances, then you'd have to sit down with a calculator and a pad of paper and figure out what you could no longer afford. And that means that you might have to deny yourself on occasion.

Well, that's just plain wrong and shouldn't happen!

So, just go on thinking that someone else will always take care of you (a husband, a wife, a mother, a father, a brother or sister or friend); or that your financial situation is the fault of George W. Bush or the globalists or the Council on Foreign Relations or your local mail carrier. It's never *your* fault no matter what happens to you, and you shouldn't have to discipline yourself—not now or ever. What kind of life would that be? A "fun" life? A life like you see in *Vogue* or *Esquire?* I don't think so, do you?

Responsibility about money is for nerds and geeks. You're a hippie, a free spirit, not an accountant. So do whatever you feel like doing, and let someone else worry about it.

# 17

## $ $ $

### Trust That There's Always More Money Coming In

Suppose you get a bonus at work. Some idiots might say that you should save it in case you really need it someday. But why? First of all, I already told you not to save, because that means you're not buying everything you want and need *right now.* But second, just because you got that one bonus, that doesn't mean there won't be another one coming along. So spend that bonus on a vacation or a boat or a new truck! You won't ever get fired. You won't ever get laid off. There will always be tons of money coming in for you to blow on toys and games.

Or, what if you get an inheritance? Great for you, I say. But for heaven's sake, don't be a stingy guy or gal and hoard it. No, the people who left it to you want you to have fun with it. That means go out and spend it.

What's that, you say? It's probably the only inheritance you'll ever get and you'd better sock it away? Uh, I don't think so. I think it would be much more prudent to spend it like a drunken sailor and have faith that somewhere out yonder there's some other generous relation who's also going to leave you a chunk of change. So please don't worry that there will ever be a lack of money—it will never happen!

Where might you get that chunk of change you might need? Well, can you spell L-O-T-T-E-R-Y?

# 18

## $ $ $

### Lend Money to Your Friends— Especially Your Girlfriend or Boyfriend

Remember that line from *Hamlet* where Polonius said: "Neither a borrower nor a lender be"? Well, maybe that made sense 400 or so years ago when Shakespeare wrote it, but it's a bunch of baloney today.

Lending money is a good thing. As you well know, lending money binds you together with your friends. It keeps them close. It says that you care. Plus, it shows that you have enough confidence in yourself to part with the money. And most of all, lending money to your friends lets them know that you trust them to pay you back.

And this is true in spades when it comes to your significant others! You want to show them you care, so naturally you'd want to lend them money. This is a genuinely kind thing to do, and it will make them love you even more than they do now. When they pay you back—as they inevitably will—you'll thank them profusely, they'll be eternally grateful, and you'll be even better friends and lovers—even more so than if you'd given them a diamond necklace or an SUV.

They'll be touched that you parted with the money—if only for a brief moment until you got paid back—and *you* will be heartened that they paid you back so promptly and lovingly.

The beautiful part about all this is that history supports the position that you'll get paid back. Lovers always repay money. Those sad sacks you see on *Judge Judy* who didn't pay back their lovers? They're one in a million. Don't even think about them at all. Love means that you always get paid back, and that your love affair will be even stronger after the transaction is completed.

So go for it, trusted reader. Cement those ties and bind them in granite by lending money to friends and lovers.

# 19

## $ $ $

## Learn the Ultimate Rule of Success—Money Spent on Appearances Is the Best Money You Can Spend!

Money attracts money. That's an old and very true adage. But suppose you don't have a lot of money to start with? Well, the only way to fool that old money god is to pretend that you *do* have a lot of cash. That means, very specifically, that you must, must, must dress and drive as if you've got some dough. If you wear Armani or Polo, you'll attract other people who wear those labels. They will no doubt be rich, and somehow just by being in their presence, *you* will get rich, too. Similarly, if you drive a Jaguar or a BMW convertible, *you* will be a magnet for those who drive those cars, and they will make you rich as well.

In other words, look and dress the part, and you'll soon be surrounded by other rich people who will start pouring money down on your little head.

Money spent in this manner is far better than saving could ever be. It is, after all, an investment in your future. Great things happen to people who put on the façade. It's that simple. And for heaven's sake, don't start worrying again about how much anything costs. . . . How many times do I have to spell C-R-E-D-I-T C-A-R-D?!

# 20

## $ $ $

### Play Lady—or Lord—Bountiful by Shelling Out Money to Everyone Around You

Do you have some sad-sack friends who are always broke? Good! Then take them out shopping and buy them all of the clothing, accessories, and electronic gadgets they need!

Are a bunch of your pals gathering for lunch? Great! Charge the whole meal on your credit card.

Do you have some neighbors who need some cheering up? Fabulous. Buy them something wildly extravagant like diamond jewelry or a membership to a country club.

Do you know some unfortunate souls who have been laid off from their jobs? Oh, that's so sad. Don't just offer to pay their rent—buy them a car. Show that you're the lord of the manor and the one who has money to burn when your friends are in trouble.

Doing so performs the dual function of helping out with the finances of the unfortunate ones, and also making you feel like a big shot. Who cares if you're only a few hundred bucks behind the poor schlubs yourself? Show off anyway. It'll make you feel better, and that's all that counts. Don't worry about what will happen next month when you can't pay your bills. You're Santa Claus, and it's your job to give and give and give.

And anyhow, who doesn't feel good tossing money around as if it were just so much shredded lettuce? And don't ruin the feeling by worrying about it!

# 21

## $ $ $

## Don't Think about Retirement— It's a L-O-O-N-N-G Way Off

The truth is (and you really need to remember this), that you're young and vibrant no matter how old you might happen to be right now. You might be 20 or you might be 40 or you might be 60, but you're still light years away from retirement. In fact, it's so far down the road that you can't even see it. And you know what? You never *will* be able to see it! Time passes very slowly, and your youth, or relative youth, will go on forever. Plus, medical science is making such amazing strides that you'll be biking 20 miles a day and playing five sets of tennis until you're 100.

So why do you need to think about what you're going to live on when you're old and retired?

It ain't gonna happen for, well . . . forever. And you'll be totally prepared when the time comes anyway. How? Well, for one thing, the U.S. government will take care of you. Or your relatives or friends will give you money. Or just by virtue of being 65 years old, somehow money will appear from nowhere even though you never invested in anything and have no savings.

Don't you remember how I told you that someone else is always responsible for you? That's true! So don't you worry about a thing.

Just to summarize: First, you won't ever get old. Second, you won't ever have to worry about money. And third, someone else will always take care of you. It's all too boring to even think about it, so don't. Plus, it's really fun to be old and not have any money. It gives you the opportunity for fantasy and invention and trying new things . . . like poverty.

Retirement? Yawn. It just takes care of itself.

$$\$ \, \$ \, \$$

Now, let's change gears a bit. Remember how I told you that you shouldn't save anything or worry about your future? After all, it puts lines on your face.

But what if someone has talked you into worrying about money? What if some fool has made you believe that you should invest in stocks or bonds or an IRA? Well, all right. I guess there are some people who can be talked into anything!

But let me give you a few words of advice if you've actually started to begin some kind of investment plan. This is important, so listen up . . .

# 22

## $ $ $

## Choose a Broker Based on His (or Her) Good Looks, Fashion Sense, and Gift of Gab

That's the way to choose a stockbroker! After all, how could he have gotten the money for that nice suit or those handsome cuff links if he weren't a star performer in the investment area? How could he always wear those snazzy Hermès ties if he didn't really know his way around the financial world? And don't you find that good-looking people are almost always well-to-do and tend to be smarter than those who are just average-looking? This means that if you can find a broker who's super attractive and put together, he'll undoubtedly know a lot more about stocks than one who's just an ordinary schmoe.

To put it more succinctly, if your broker's a looker, is nattily attired, and is in the finance business, he's obviously made a ton of money for himself . . . and probably for his clients, too. That means he'll make a lot of money for you as well, and then you'll also find yourself hobnobbing at The Polo Club and The Yacht Club and those other places where he hangs out.

The world of finance is a tricky, complex world, so what you want is someone who's smooth-talking and confident. Your broker has to be able to convince you that he can do great things with your money by putting it in junk bonds and other areas too arcane for you to know about personally.

But please don't make the mistake of asking your broker (or potential broker)—just what kind of education he has. Similarly, it would be rude and tasteless to ask him to give you references from satisfied clients. All you need to see is that he's wearing an Armani suit, a Rolex, and Gucci shoes—and then you can breathe a sigh of relief because you know that your hard-earned money will be in good hands.

Another thing: Don't look for nerds and brainiacs when you're shopping for a broker. They may do very well in the classroom, but they're not going to do at all well in the "real world" where savoir faire, toughness, and street smarts combine to (mysteriously) produce an elegantly coiffed stock-market wizard.

And don't hire anyone old or rumpled or boxy looking, or someone who spends his spare time, say, playing bridge instead of downing martinis and spinning the roulette wheel. Basically, look for someone who could be a *GQ* cover boy—that is, someone like Pierce Brosnan and not, well, like Warren Buffett.

# 23

## $ $ $

## Attend a "Free" Financial Seminar, and Follow the Advice They "Sell" You to the Letter

Figure it out. If the people who are putting on these seminars are doing it for free, how bad a deal can it be? And how very sure of themselves they must be to offer their advice gratis and just let the merits of their plans and schemes sell themselves, so to speak. There are super-strict government requirements (aren't there?) regulating who can put on these seminars, so the individuals giving the one you're attending wouldn't have even been allowed to do anything that important unless they'd met the most stringent financial, educational, ethical, and legal standards.

This means that you can trust every single word they say. If they tell you they have a "system" or a "program" that's "guaranteed" to produce immense wealth, then rest assured that the Federal Trade Commission (FTC) wouldn't have allowed them to make those claims unless they were true. I can tell you this for sure because I (your author) used to be a lawyer with the FTC, and I definitely saw the beady eyes of those government gumshoes scanning the horizon for every kind of scam—and the ones they unearthed were shut down instantly.

The same thing happens at the Securities and Exchange Commission (SEC). If you can't trust the federal government to look out for your best interests where securities sales are concerned, you can't trust much, and I pity you. (Remember, these are the same people who scouted out Enron and Global Crossing before they did any damage. Now you can relax.)

So, go on, take that free financial seminar! The organizers are good guys and gals who just want you to be wealthy. Join up with them, have a good time, get rich quick, and then maybe you can have a few drinks with them at their next carnival show—oops, I mean seminar.

# 24

## $ $ $

### Make a Point of Watching Those Late-Night Financial Success Infomercials

Are you an insomniac? Maybe you work odd shifts and rarely get to bed before three in the morning, or perhaps you're just a clever dog and know how the world works. There's an old Italian saying that goes something like this: *Money is made at night.* Now, this used to mean that money was often gotten illegally and had to be made while the sun didn't shine and people couldn't see what was going on.

But there's a different meaning these days. Nowadays, real wealth is made by those who wait up until midnight or later and then watch infomercials telling them how to make money.

Why are these shows on so late at night? Oh, silly you! Because if they were on in the middle of the day, everyone in the world would watch them and learn all the secrets of making a fortune from nothing, and soon everybody would be taking advantage of those deals. After all, how many gorgeous, pristine homes are there in bankruptcy that you can buy with no money down? If the shows that told you how to acquire them were on at 6 P.M. on CBS, they'd all be snapped up.

So the late bird gets the worm in this case. The late bird gets to stay up late, see what's what in the world of finance, and make real money while all the rest of us lazy slobs are sleeping.

Now, it may seem to you that the people on these shows are a bit vague about how they acquired all those yachts and polo ponies. But that's because, again, the information they're disseminating is classified and is intended only for the eyes and ears of those smart enough to stay up late and watch TV.

Pity those poor fools who think Ben Franklin knew what he was talking about. You know the *real* way to be healthy, wealthy, and wise: Stay up late, pay attention to the "wealth-building program" of the evening, and be happy.

# 25

## $ $ $

# Rest Assured That If a Person Is Quoted in *The Wall Street Journal* or on TV, She (or He) Must Be Able to Forecast the Stock Market

It ain't easy to get on TV. Just ask anyone. That means, in a nutshell, that if someone gets on air to talk about the stock market, she must have passed rigorous government and private tests that gauge her ability to predict what's going to happen. The TV shows keep close track of every syllable that she ever says about the market. These words are then compared with how the market actually did. A precise correlation is made on complex graphs and top-secret computers.

Anyone who doesn't live up to very strict standards is immediately bounced right off the airwaves. If, for instance, a stock-market analyst told you that tech stocks were the ticket to wealth and riches back in March of 2000 before the Crash, that person would be immediately banned from all network- and cable-TV news and financial programs. The TV stations and networks have reputations to protect, and they cannot guard those reputations if they don't assiduously check to make sure that every "expert" they put on the air is consistently right.

So rest assured that if someone appears on a TV show and talks about the stock market, you can be very, very certain that she knows what the heck she's talking about, and you'll make jillions just by heeding her advice.

The same is true for the financial press. Magazines and newspapers such as *Fortune* or *Business Week* or *The Wall Street Journal* closely follow every prediction and pontification of every person they quote. This means that they screen carefully for those who have made mistakes in the past and ban them forever from their pages if they've been found wanting. For example, if someone ever said that the stock market was fairly priced when the Dow was 12,000 and was going far higher in the future . . . and then it fell to 7,500 . . . an account would be kept, and those people would not be allowed to dispense any advice in the future. If they said that you should get out of real estate and into stocks when the NASDAQ was about to fall by 80 percent, they would never be called upon for their words of "wisdom" again.

So know that you can abide by the information given by anyone who has ever appeared on TV or in the financial press. These "experts" know what they're doing, and if they didn't, how could they be associated with such prominent broadcast and print organizations?

Yup. They really know their stuff.

# 26

## $ $ $

## Don't Pay Any Attention to Financial Experts who Urge You to Diversify—the Stock Market Is Always the Best (and Only) Place to Be!

Hey, the long-term trend of the stock market is always up, up, and away. I mean, the Dow has risen from about 40 in 1933, to about 9,600 as I write this in 2003, so just look at the curve, man! That doesn't even count dividends. Just a few thousand socked away in the depths of the Great Depression would translate to millions nowadays.

The fact is that all of the smart people know that the long term will bail you out in the stock market and will make you rich. So stay in it and keep adding to it all the time. And whatever you do, don't spread your money around and put it into anything else.

Some mean-spirited, grumpy people such as Alan Abelson (a financial columnist for *Barron's*) might warn you that there have been long periods when the stock market has gone way, way down. They might tell you that even in postwar periods, there have been decades when the stock market hardly moved at all in an upward direction.

*Do not believe them!* Forget about the crash of 1987. Forget about the disasters in 1973 and '74. Don't pay any attention to the fact that it took the stock market 25 years after 1929 to reach its 1929 level again; or that adjusted for inflation, it took the market more than 50 years to reach its 1929 level again—or that the NASDAQ had the worst stock-market plunge in postwar history just a few years ago.

The people who tell you these things are just party-pooping spoil sports. Don't pay any attention to them. The truth is that all of these little blips may have happened, but they're just tiny eddies and cross-currents in a majestic river flow of progress, prosperity, and upward movement in the stock market.

You're never going to have any use for the money you've invested in the market during a time when the market has tanked, so don't worry about that! And you're *not* going to die right in the middle of a crash or have to retire or have to pay for emergency medical care. You can afford to wait forever for the market to recover if things turn sour!

So, while those grouchy curmudgeons like Alan Abelson keep warning you, you just keep ignoring what they say while you grow richer and richer. Ha! Experience counts for very little in the stock market, my friend. Just buy, buy, buy.

# 27

## $ $ $

## Convince Yourself That You Can Beat the Market without Knowing Anything about It

What, after all, does someone like *you* even have to know about the market? The nerds and geeks may have graduate degrees. Some money managers may have decades of experience. Some pundits like Warren Buffett may have an abundance of both. But *you* have your innate gambler's luck and feel—the only cards you'll ever need. You can tell just by the way you get out of bed in the morning in which direction the market is headed. You can tell by the way the numbers are running across your computer screen whether it's an up day or a down day. You don't need a system or education or information gleaned from late hours of study—you have that feeling in your fingertips. Call it instinct, call it luck, or call it by its rightful name: genius. You can forecast the market just by the feeling in your bones.

And individual stocks? You don't need to learn how to read a 10-K or an S-1 or whatever the heck those things with the tiny little type are called. You don't have to know anything at all about accounting. Economics? Marketing? Research on business cycles or specific industries? Nonsense! Just by hearing a company's *name* you can tell if it's a winner or a loser—the same way you pick horses at the racetrack. Don't be a slave to some musty old library or some ponderous old computer. Just plunk down your money right this minute based on pure intuition.

This is definitely the way to play the market, and your way is the best way. While the other schnooks are plodding around with their tables and charts, you'll be making millions, 'cause you've got that lucky streak going—not to mention the unshakable conviction that you're always right. And that's more than enough.

# 28

## $ $ $

## Carve It in Stone: "Average" Returns in the Stock Market Aren't Good Enough for You!

Now, it may be true that very few of the world's money managers ever manage to "beat the market"—that is, earn better returns than the market does as a whole. There are, in fact, many scholarly studies around that prove this is true. In fact, I will go a little further and say that it may be true that even great financial geniuses can't "beat the market" for long periods. But *you* can and will, just by virtue of what you've got in the marrow of your bones!

Why should you be satisfied with "average" returns that mimic the stock market's overall trends? You're a lot better than average in every other aspect of your life (at least you think you are). So why settle for average by buying an index fund where the managers basically purchase all the big stocks in the market and then you just sit back and watch?

That might be fine for a passive, lazybones couch potato. But that ain't you. Not by a long shot. You're the kind of person who thrives on a challenge. Yes, it may be true that index funds and large (very large) mutual funds like Fidelity Magellan beat the results the ordinary small investor gets about 80 percent of the time. But so what? That has nothing to do with you.

So, don't do the easy, path-of-least-resistance thing. Get yourself psyched up to try all kinds of tricks and strategies to actually "beat the market." You're a world-beating, market-beating genius with more tricks than a dog has fleas.

And here are a few more of them. . . .

# 29

## $ $ $

### Don't Waste Your Time with a Broker Who Works for a Well-Known Firm—Go with That Nimble Little Fellow Who Sent You Spam on the Internet

The big boys, the Merrill Lynches, the Smith Barneys, the Prudentials—they're all just fossils. You need someone small and hip who can wheel and deal in and among the big old whales. You need a wily, agile guy who needs to make his bones by making you rich. That, at least to me, means someone who sent you an e-mail or a fax or maybe called you up. This is someone who isn't rich yet, but he's trying to *make* himself rich, and the only way he can do that is to make *you* rich, and then you'll tell your pals, and they'll tell *their* pals, and soon you'll all be rich.

There are some naysayers who will probably tell you that you can't trust those who make cold calls and who send you spam on the Internet. After all, who can verify their names and their reputations? But that is precisely the point, my dear friend. They are the underdogs who can spot the big opportunities before the major brokerage houses have gotten off their keesters (after their two-hour martini lunches).

So put your trust in that little guy, make him really work for you, and watch that money grow, grow, grow. Oh, by the way, haven't you ever heard of the SEC? I mentioned them a few pages back. They're on the job like white on rice, making sure that every single word sent by fax or over the Internet is totally correct and by the book. Once again, if you can't trust the government to look after you, who *can* you trust?

# 30

## $ $ $

## Act Fast! Those Stock Tips You Heard about in the Locker Room Have Real Value

I think all of us know someone who's gotten rich on a stock tip, don't we? I mean, how can we little guys (and gals) ever get to the big time if we don't act on tips and get a leg up on the competition? We don't have huge research departments. We don't have connections at the country club. No . . . but we do have friends who *hear things*. And every so often, if we're really lucky, we can *overhear* some of those things and get ourselves really well positioned to make megabucks.

Don't bother to ask how your source knows what he knows. Don't look a gift horse in the mouth by inquiring about whether any of his other "hot tips" made any money. And please don't rack your brain trying to remember if anyone ever *did* make any money as a result of a stock tip (without also going to jail, that is). No, just plunge in, and then you can laugh at all of those saps who made investments based on research and hard work while you're swimming laps in your heated Olympic-size pool.

# 31

## $ $ $

## Don't Be Satisfied to Just Buy and Hold—Rapid Trading Is the Key to Wealth

If you've ever seen a movie about Wall Street (*Wall Street* is a good one!), you know very well that at the heart of this city within a city lurk men and women slaving at computer consoles, holding one phone up to each ear, shrieking "Buy!" or "Sell!" This frantic pace exemplifies how money is made in this world. It has little indeed to do with cautiously buying and holding.

Have you ever seen a movie about wealthy people on Wall Street who just sit quietly reading a novel while the investments they made ten years ago slowly grow in value? No, I don't think you have, and I don't think you ever will.

Clearly, as you can see in movies and TV programs about the stock market, real money is made by trading frequently.

Think about it: How many people do you know who have quit their day jobs and then gotten rich just trading online a few hours each day at home with no guidance except the innate genius they were born with? Hundreds, I'm sure!

Buy and hold may have been fine for your grandfather's investments, but this isn't your grandfather's market. This is the new, fast-paced world of tomorrow, and you can either be in it or out of it, either make money by furious trading, or just be content being average by buying the indexes and large mutual funds and watching your life drift by down that ol' lazy river.

Some nitwits are probably going to say that there's a big difference between the way that major banks and brokerages trade, and the way that you would do it as an individual. They'll probably say that the big banks and brokerages have hedges, immense capital backing them up, and far more information than you'll ever be able to access.

Nonsense. The computer and the Internet are the great equalizers. You can do everything the big boys can do . . . and do it better and more nimbly (possibly with help from your spam-sending broker at a no-name firm!).

Don't be scared off by those horror stories about people who traded actively and lost everything. That will not happen to you. You have luck and (in fact) genius on your side, and they don't. Plus, they are not you, and that makes all the difference in the world.

# 32

## $ $ $

## Invest in Penny Stocks

Look at it this way. Suppose you buy stock in a totally unknown company, XYZ Technologies, and it's selling over the Internet for $.50 a share. Then, suppose it goes up by $.25. That means it's gone up by 50 percent—and that's real moolah!

On the other hand, if you buy GE, a company everyone is already bored with, at, say, $25, and it goes up by $.25, you've only made one percent. How are you going to make any real money that way?

Simple answer: You can't and you won't. But there's plenty of leverage in penny stocks. If they move just a tiny bit, you make a fortune. And don't worry that the same principle also works in reverse. That is, if you buy GE at $25 and it goes down by $.50, you've lost 2 percent, but if you buy XYZ at $.50 and it goes down by $.50, you've lost 100 percent.

This will never happen to you, though, because you're only buying really top-quality penny stocks, the GEs and GMs of the penny stocks—only they haven't been discovered yet.

Plus, you're only buying after you've gotten really hot tips, and when you know for sure that you're going to watch that stock zoom into the stratosphere.

So, go ahead. Live a little, pal. Swing with the penny stocks and ignore the possible pitfalls while you're riding in your pink Cadillac.

# 33

## $ $ $

## To Make Real Money, Go on Margin!

You may have never heard of "margin" except for the margins on the pages when you were taking typing class. But "margin" is an incredibly kind invention created by brokers to help make you rich.

Basically, when you "go on margin," you're borrowing money from your broker to buy extra stock you wouldn't be able to buy if you just had to pay cash for all of the stock you bought. For example, suppose you want to buy 1,000 shares of XYZ at 28, but you only have $20,000. The broker will usually lend you the other $8,000. Now, to be sure, you have to pay interest on that loan, and the interest is usually at a pretty hefty rate. But never mind that. The real truth is that you're borrowing in order to buy a stock that you and your broker just *know* will go up in value. You know it for sure. And it's bound to go up in value a lot more than the paltry interest you're paying for it, even though the interest might not seem at first blush to be so tiny on that margin account.

To clarify, if your money-market account at your brokerage house is paying eight-tenths of one percent, which is what the broker pays you when you lend him money in late 2003, that same broker will usually charge you about 7 percent to go on margin, or about nine times as much. To some whiners, that might seem like a lot. But for a smart investor like you, the story is far more apparent.

You're borrowing at 7 percent to buy a stock that you just know will double in value imminently. If that stock goes up by 100 percent, you will have only paid 7 percent to make 100 percent, leaving you with a nifty 93 percent profit—and if the stock goes up by 100 percent in a few weeks, as your picks usually will (!), you don't even have to pay all of the 7 percent margin interest. You just pay for however many days you used a 7 percent annual rate.

That means you can and do fatten your profits immensely by going on margin. It's a gift from the brokerage community. In fact, it's almost like charity.

It can get even better, though. If you're buying high-tech or biotech stocks that really swing, they can move up 200 to 300 percent in a few months—so think of the money you could make! If you just put down the minimum in cash and have all of the rest as margin (or borrowed funds), you can put rocket fuel into your portfolio. Under regulations in force as I write this, you can borrow roughly up to 50 percent of your purchase on margin.

This means you can buy twice as much as you would otherwise have bought if you'd just done the ordinary thing—that is, pay cash. *How great is that?!*

Now, as always, there will be some grouches and naysayers—I tell you, they're everywhere—who might warn you that the stock you buy is security for your margin borrowings, and if the stock falls by more than about 10 percent, you'll get an ugly thing called a "margin call." This is a phone call early in the morning that demands that you put up more money to make up for the fall in the value of your stock. That call might tell you that if you don't put up the cash right away, your position will be sold out and you'll still be liable for any difference between what you owe on the stock and what the sale brought in.

Now, some may say that they recall that in the Crash of 2000 to 2002, people who went heavily on margin ended up getting margin calls for their crashing tech stocks, couldn't come up with the cash, had the stock sold out from under them, still didn't have the funds to make up the difference, and had to sell their houses to raise the money for the margin they still owed on stocks that had become worthless or almost worthless.

But that won't ever happen to *you,* pal! You don't buy stocks that go down. You buy stocks that go up, up, and away! You'll never need to worry about a margin call because you're Mr. Lucky, and your stocks will never get closer to earth—only closer to the sun!

So, go on margin, have a great time with it, and drop me a note from your villa on the Riviera letting me know how you're doing!

# 34

## $ $ $

### Believe in "Black Box" Trading Methods Pitched to You by Some Wizard in a Fancy Suit

You know, there's a famous saying that goes something like this: If you're so smart, why ain't you rich? The obvious meaning of this is that smart people are rich—and know how to make *you* rich. This means that investing is, in some small way, an art, but it's largely a science. Precise scientific methods like the ones that landed a man on the moon are what we need to make the real bucks. Astrophysicists, research scientists, mathematicians who delve into quantum physics—these are the guys and gals who can make us wealthy.

So if these geniuses have some proprietary, mathematics-crammed "black box" that harnesses the power of math and the other sciences to tame the market's wild beast and make us rich in the process, why should we shy away from such a marvel? Simple answer? We shouldn't! We should grab for the gusto with both hands.

Don't worry yourself thinking about some company in Connecticut called Long-Term Capital Management and how their "black-box" methods led to a loss of billions of dollars. Don't worry about other investors who've lost their shirts to "black-box" methods that turned out to be highly fallible to say the least. *Your* black box is going to work because it's yours . . . and it's black . . . and it's a box!

# 35

## $ $ $

## Put All Your Eggs in One Basket— 'Cause Only Sissies Diversify

Now, get this straight. You, with the help of that broker you met on the Internet, your margin calls, and your innate luck, are not about to pick stocks that go down. Yours are going *up*. Knowing that, what's the point of diluting your attention and your gains by diversifying and buying lots of different stocks? Why give yourself a lot of confusing things to think about and a lot of extra lines on your financial statements?

No, put all of your eggs in that basket that's marked "For Winners Only"! Maybe do the thing that's easiest and involves the path of least resistance: Put all of your money into the stock of the company that employs you. Often, that company will sell you its stock at a bargain rate, considerably below the market price. And you know it's a good company—otherwise you wouldn't be there, you dog, you! So, yes, definitely put all of your eggs in that one basket and watch them hatch and turn out golden geese!

Diversification? We don't need no stinkin' diversification!

# 36

## $ $ $

## Ignore Investment Fees and Expenses—They're Just Nickels and Dimes

So what if your mutual fund charges you 6 percent or 4 percent or 3 percent to get into it. Who the heck cares? Those are just a few pennies out of every dollar. So what if you could've bought an almost identical mutual fund for "no load" (no fees) or no commission on the sale at all? These are just tiny sums. They'll never add up to a thing.

And so what if your broker is charging you 2 percent on the price of the stocks with a $200 minimum charge? That's just 2 percent out of every dollar. When your stock has doubled, you won't remember the cost of that commission one little bit.

None of those costs will ever add up to a thing compared with the billions you'll make on your investments. So just pay whatever the brokers or the mutual funds charge. Hey, they have to eat, too, right? And you want them to be happy and fat and sleek; otherwise, how will they ever be in a good enough mood to make any real money for you? (And don't worry about such esoterica and trivia as "market timing" or "late trading" by the managers of your mutual funds. They may look unethical and crooked, but that's just because you are innocent and naive. There's really nothing at all wrong with any of those things, so don't worry your pretty little head about it.)

Worrywarts and nerds and prissy-pants investors worry about those few cents on the dollar that go toward fees and charges. But swingin' cats like you who make billions and live in mansions and cruise on yachts didn't get there by worrying about a few cents here and there.

Hey, if you're going to worry about every nickel and dime, maybe you shouldn't be investing your money at all!

# 37

## $ $ $

### Buy and Read Newsletters about Investing, and Do Exactly What They Say

Publishing a newsletter about the stock market is no small feat. It takes a hefty amount of knowledge, education, experience, and street savvy. They don't let just *anyone* do these things. You have to be someone who's been around the market a long time and has made tons of money consistently for oneself and for one's readers—only then will the FTC or the SEC (or whoever regulates newsletters) allow the guy or gal to write and sell the publication.

You can trust anyone who passes this rigorous test and believe every word he writes.

Wait just a freaking minute! What's that, you say? You heard that there *are basically no* FTC or SEC regulations for people writing and publishing financial newsletters? That anyone can do it anytime he or she feels like it? Well, maybe, but so what? They do have to fill out some forms, don't they? Isn't that enough?

The investment business is populated by men and women of only the highest moral character. Those who take on the awesome responsibility of advising others would not do so lightly. They would have to feel in their heart and soul that they could do the job properly, that they had the right credentials, and that they had a long history of making money in all kinds of markets.

And so what if the "data" shows that newsletter writers are usually wrong and, in fact, you can usually make more money by doing just the opposite of what they advise?

Well, none of this applies to you . . . *because you're only going to read the newsletter that's always right.* And how will you know which one that is? Never mind. You'll just know. So go ahead and read to your heart's content, and plunk down your very last dime investing in what the writers recommend. You'll be up there with the Rockefellers in no time flat!

# 38

## $ $ $

## Make Sure You Never Hold Your Financial Adviser or Broker Accountable—You Want Him to Be Your Friend

There are measurements that come out regularly in *Barron's, The Wall Street Journal,* and many other fine financial publications about how well the stock market has done in the past six months, the past year, or the past five years. They track broad market indexes like the S&P 500 and the Dow Jones 30 Industrials.

Please don't make your financial adviser's life difficult by comparing his picks and suggestions with this broad gauge. You only need to know that he's your pal, that he takes your calls promptly, and basically, that's it. If he's a friend to you, talks to you, reassures you, and maybe occasionally takes you to lunch and picks up the tab, you know he's your kind of guy. Don't make him feel bad if other measurements are going up faster than your investments. He's a nice family man with a good personality. That's enough.

# 39

## $ $ $

## If Your Investment Program Isn't Producing Good Results, Keep Doing the Same Thing Anyway

You might have heard the old saying, "If nothing changes, then nothing changes." That means that if you keep doing what you've *been* doing, then you'll get the same results you've always gotten.

Some might tell you that this applies in spades to your investments. If you keep doing the same thing, you might keep getting the same results. But, that's not true for you. If by some weird fluke your investments (recommended by your no-name broker, your friends on the Internet, newsletter writers, infomercial spokespersons, and the tips you overheard at the gym) don't do well for a few years, just keep doing the same thing—that is, investing based on suggestions from those same sources—and sure enough, those investments will turn the corner and start rocketing up.

With the exception of the ones that have gone bankrupt and stopped trading, of course. Those probably won't recover, but for you, they might come back and start dancing on their graves and make you some money.

So just go with the flow, and don't worry, be happy. Wait a few more years to check on how you're doing. In the meantime, let it flow, let it flow.

And this leads to the next item, as vital as any other for ruining your financial life . . .

# 40

## $ $ $

## If Taking Charge of Your Financial Life Seems Overwhelming Now, Just Put It Off for a Few More Years

There's this old myth that says you should get movin' right now on accomplishing your goals, because the more time you have to work on them, the more likely you are to attain them. And then there's some old saw about how a journey is more likely to get finished if you start early in the morning.

What a load of bull! Didn't the idiots who came up with those maxims realize how much fun it is to sleep late? Didn't they know that some days are just for kicking back and having a few martinis and watching the sunset?

It takes a lot of mental effort to take charge of your finances. If it seems a bit burdensome right now, just wait a while until it seems like it would be less of a bother. Only when you're really and truly up to it should you get yourself in gear to make plans for your financial future. Don't worry about the time that passed while you were getting yourself organized. I'm sure it was good for something—if only for sleeping late, you movie star, you!

# 41

## $ $ $

## Start a Business with Inadequate Capital—in a Difficult Field and in a Difficult Location— and Expect to Prosper

This essay could just as well be called "Open a Restaurant," which is surely one of the best ways on earth to lose a ton of money, your spouse, and your peace of mind. But don't let that thought worry you. No, forget what I just wrote. I was just kidding.

But, seriously, why don't you open a restaurant in an area where millions of other people have started eateries that went out of business. Go ahead. It'll be fine. Where everyone else—even people with experience—went down the tubes, you'll succeed just because of your innate charisma.

Besides, restaurants are really easy businesses to run. I mean, haven't you ever seen *Casablanca?* Humphrey Bogart is always in a dinner jacket or a suit, is never in a hurry, and never has to face problems with customers or waiters who don't show up or waitresses who have to leave early for an audition. Owners of restaurants lead care-free lives, just lounging on the chaise while the money rolls in on top of them.

So start a restaurant—or any business where the failure rate is 90 percent or more—and you'll be amazed to see how easy and fun it is and how much money you make. You won't need to worry about burning through all your cash in a few months and being overwhelmed by debt. Nope, not you—'cause you won't make the same mistakes those other suckers made.

You know better.

# 42

## $ $ $

# Don't Worry about Buying Stocks when There's a Bubble Going On—You'll Always Know when to Sell Out Just Before the Bubble Bursts

There are a lot of old-fashioned measurements that tell old fogeys when stocks are cheap and when they're expensive by historic measurements. These are ways to calculate the ratio of the stock's price with respect to its earnings and dividends. When these get really, really high—when stocks are flying—those measurements are really high, too, and some curmudgeons call those times "bubbles" and tell you to stay away from buying stocks then.

What nonsense that is! When stocks are high-flyin', that's when it's the most fun to be in the stock market! How much fun is it to invest when stocks barely move at all, or at most, a few percent a year? It's BO-RING. But when stocks are really soaring, and when they've cut their ties to history and earth and common sense, that's when you pick up the stock page of the newspaper or go online and find out that your tech stock has doubled within the last week. That's when you really feel super-duper rich and smart.

So, why listen to the old creeps who tell you to beware when the stock market is at those levels? Why even pay a moment's attention? If, in fact, the bubble is bound to burst, you'll know about it and get out in plenty of time.

Uh, *how* will you know? Well, hasn't Warren Buffett said that in a bubble, everyone says they'll leave the party at midnight, only there are no clocks in the room? Yes, but so what? You don't invest based on clocks and old fuddy-duddy rules. You invest by the intuitive feelings in your fingertips, and those feelings will also tell you when—exactly when—to sell, take your profits, and go hang out at Cap d'Antibes.

So, go ahead. Buy at the peak. You'll never regret it, not for a moment. Bubbles are fun for you because you, and only you, know when to get in and when to get out.

Now, let's leave the stock market and investing behind. After all, the market isn't the only game in town. Let's try some other ways for you to get rich quick (and ruin your financial life). . . .

# 43

## $ $ $

### If Getting Your Finances Together Seems Too Difficult at Any Given Time, Turn Everything Over to a Financial/Business Manager Who Will Have Total Control Over Your Money

Hey, why worry about nickels and dimes and boring things like IRAs and Keoghs and how much money to save? Why fill out dusty old forms for the IRS or the state income-tax board? Why not have some gal with a green eyeshade and sleeve garters take care of all that for you?

My advice is to find some trustworthy person who claims to be well versed in money management, go to her office with your checkbook and a power of attorney, and turn everything over to her. In this world, you can only trust a few select people with your money, but you'll unerringly find the right one. A suggestion? Go for the one who charges the most. Don't be happy with anyone who charges you less than 5 percent. Maybe even pay a few percentage points more for quality service.

Then, just send all your bills to her and have her pay them, let her withdraw money from your accounts for investments, and generally allow her to do everything but the heavy lifting. And don't feel lazy for doing it. Many busy, important people like you have better things to do than worry about stuffy old money matters.

You may have heard those horror stories about financial managers who looted their clients mainly because these folks were too lazy to pay any attention to their financial statements. You may have also heard stories about horribly mangled billing statements from credit-card companies and department stores that some business manager's semiliterate assistant paid anyway and the money could never be recovered. You may have heard of financial managers who made terrible mistakes in their investment decisions for one client and then looted their other clients to cover it up.

Pay no attention to any of this at all. It will never happen to you. If you can't trust someone with a nice office and a smooth patter to handle your money, who can you trust?

Besides, untended pots of money are not really *that* big a temptation to wicked minds, are they? Certainly not. So go right ahead and live it up while your financial manager takes over the reins. There will never be a day of reckoning for trusting your future to someone whose interests might totally differ from yours and who might have the ethics of a snake.

And if you believe that one . . .

# 44

## $ $ $

# Believe That You Can Get Rich Quick—That You Can Get Something for Nothing

There *are* such things as free lunches!

This one is so obvious that I don't think I need to say much about it. It's simply a statement of truth that a smart guy or gal like you was born knowing.

Basically, real riches appear overnight just by luck or chance or a bolt of inspiration (see the next essay). You don't need to trade experience or labor or investments for wealth. If you're on the right track, you'll reap the financial rewards overnight . . . money will rain down on your house in torrents.

Let me explain this a little further . . .

# 45

## $$$

## Know Without a Doubt That You Don't Have to Work Hard— You Only Need to Find an Angle

Get hip to life. Hard work is for suckers. Manual labor is for losers and fools. How often have you seen impecunious (look it up) old people who have worked and slaved all of their lives and are still broke? Or at least not rich. And how many of your pals work year in and year out and just get tiny little pay raises (or none at all) and never get ahead?

The truth of this realization is painful but then liberating: *Hard work gets you nowhere slowly.* It's for those without imagination.

But *you* are different. You have that creative spark. You have that special magic that's going to make you wake up one morning at 4 A.M., shout out, "Eureka!" and have the brainstorm that will bring you staggering wealth.

What will the inspiration be? Well, if I knew, I'd be as rich as you're going to be, wouldn't I? And I'm not, am I? So what will it be? The next Velcro? A new computer program that lets people actually make love through the Internet? A perfume for dogs that allows them to smell as good as they look? A dating service for sex addicts? A formula that decodes the Bible and tells you when to buy stocks and when to sell?

You may not know what will come to you just yet, but the thing to remember is that if you hang out on the sofa most of the time, watch a lot of TV reruns, eat as much junk food as you can, and maybe smoke a few bong loads . . . then the lightbulb will surely go off. All at once, you'll vault over all of those hardworking geeks who seemed as if they'd completely outpace you. You'll rocket to success in a matter of weeks.

So don't bother to work hard. Just take a lot of naps and wait for that flash of lightning to explode in your brain. The world is waiting breathlessly for you to come down from the mountaintop with your two tablets and your inspiration that will make the Ten Commandments seem comically insignificant.

Go for it. You just need that one clever angle.

# 46

## $ $ $

## Do Not Buy a Home—a Free Spirit Like You Does Not Need to Put Down Roots

Let's face it—owning a home is a heap of trouble. You have to save up for the down payment (and I think I already told you *not* to save because it takes money away from the fun stuff you'd like to spend it on, such as vacations and clothes and cars and stereo equipment). So that's a problem.

Then you have to do something really abhorrent. You have to obligate yourself to pay off a mortgage that could last as long as 30 years. That's right. You have to promise—in blood, practically—that you'll make a large payment to the bank or mortgage company every damned month for three whole decades.

How much fun is that? Who in their right mind wants to be that tied down? I don't. Do you?

And then what about the maintenance and the upkeep? If you live in a rental, all you have to do is call the super when there's a backed-up toilet. But if you own your own home, hey, pal, you have to get out the plunger yourself. If you have rats, you can't just call the landlord and yell at him. You have to get out the rat poison and the cats and go after those wicked little rodents.

And what if the roof leaks? What do you do then? Plus, there's fire insurance, flood insurance, earthquake insurance if you live in California, liability insurance—it goes on and on. Then there's painting—and I haven't even gotten to the landscaping yet, which is a major, *major* hassle all unto itself. Until you own a home, you just have no freaking clue how much work it is. In fact, it's too much work. That's the bottom line.

And have I even mentioned termites? Do you know what a disaster they can be? But they're just one small part of the burden of home ownership.

Why do it? Oh, sure, a home may go up in value and allow your small down payment to build into a huge equity pool. So what? Is that worth having to find a plumber at 7 in the morning on a Sunday?

Yes, you do get immense tax subsidies for owning a home and financing it with a mortgage. So? I already told you not to pay taxes!

It's true that for most people, their homes become their biggest asset and help cushion ups and downs in the stock market or in their jobs. But that means zero to you. You're a troubadour. A hippie. A free bird. You don't need to concern yourself with the trivialities of mundane money grubbing. You want your landlord to worry about repairs and paint and termites. *You* worry about things like whether Britney Spears will ever get back with Justin Timberlake. You worry about whether your local supermarket will start carrying that beer you like. You worry about that scratch on your car.

Let others make their stupid profits and capital gains from their homes. If they want to convert themselves into adding machines, that's their problem—not yours. Just stay ready to hit the road any old time the feeling strikes you. No home ownership for poets and prophets like you.

Nope. No way.

# 47

## $ $ $

## Feel Confident That You Can Borrow Your Way Out of Any Problem

You know how I've been telling you over and over that you don't need to save money? Well, some of you (who haven't been listening very well) may have had a sneaking little thought enter your minds: *What if I suddenly need money? How will I handle it if I don't have any money saved up?*

Good question, and it has a good answer: You *borrow* the money when you need it by getting a cash advance on your credit cards. The interest rate is only about 20 percent. Sometimes it's lower, sometimes higher, but the banks that issue credit cards are only too happy to lend you money any old time you please. Cash advances are a breeze to get and very easy to spend.

Or, go to a finance company and get a signature loan. (Remember, you don't have a home to borrow on, right?) Those unsecured loans are really great things, too. They also charge a bit of interest, but what the heck. If you need the money, who cares about the interest?

And here's a sneaky little tip: There are also special friends out there who will want to lend you money. True, many people make it a practice *not* to lend money. But not your best pals. They can and will lend you money and tide you over any rough spots. That's what they're there for. Don't even think about being too embarrassed to ask for a loan—or worrying about your buddies' discomfort over being asked. Just ask for it—in fact, even demand it! What are friends for? They've probably been boring and practical enough to save, so what's the point of saving if not to do nice things for other people? So, go for it. Your pals will be happy to oblige—it might even strengthen your friendship.

And here's another word of advice: When you get that borrowed money, *don't repay it.* Think about it for a moment. How are you any better off if you borrow a thousand bucks and then a few weeks later *repay* a thousand bucks? You're in exactly the same position you were before. But if you borrow the thousand and then don't repay it, or only repay a little of it, you've made a profit! It's like it was a gift. So, borrow, allow your pals to feel good about helping you out, and then go on your merry way.

Borrowing your way out of a jam is really the only smart maneuver. Bear this in mind!

# 48

## $ $ $

### Rest Assured That Shopping Is a Perfectly Valid Form of Emotional and Physical Exercise—whether You Need What You're Buying or Not

It feels good to shop. You go into a store, you get people to wait on you, you try things on, you see something really cute, and you buy it. And you feel like a new person. Not only that, but you get out of the house and see people. You get to call the shots because *you're* the one throwing money around while simpering lackeys cater to your every whim.

Plus, you get exercise walking from store to store. That's good for those buttocks, calves, and thighs, dontcha know.

And while we're at it, please keep in mind a

few additional points on why shopping is so beneficial for you:

- Goods bought at retail have some value and cost something, but goods bought on sale at steep discounts are free!

- Clothes bearing fancy labels are far better than those with generic brand names—even if they look exactly the same and have the identical fabric content. And designer clothes bought in one of those brand-names-for-less stores shouldn't even be considered. Only clothes you buy at full price are worth holding on to for a long time.

- Don't stop to think about whether you really need all the items you're splurging on, on any particular day. If you like something and it fits, it means you need it and should buy it.

Sold!

# 49

## $ $ $

## Carefully Pore Over All Those Catalogs You Get in the Mail, and Order from Them Late at Night or When You're Feeling Lonely

You can really cheer your bad self up by ordering something when you're alone at home at night. Maybe your girlfriend or boyfriend just gave you a hard time (perhaps by asking for that money back that you borrowed last month). Maybe you're feeling a little down in the dumps as you lie in bed and pet your kitty. But don't worry. Just call up the catalog companies and buy some things you don't really need. The customer-service agents at those companies will be overjoyed to help you out, and they'll treat you with the respect you deserve after a hard day.

Not only that, but if it's really late at night, you'll have someone with a friendly voice to chat with!

Who cares if you don't even bother to open the boxes once they're delivered? As long as you know that those items are waiting patiently in your garage or closet for you, that's all that matters. You can get to them someday when you're good and ready, and it will be like Christmas in the middle of May.

And the real pleasure of catalog ordering isn't actually getting the merchandise. It's ordering it—and once you've done that, you can sleep like a baby. (Until you get the bill, that is.)

# 50

## $ $ $

### Don't Sweat the Small Stuff— After All, $10 or $20 a Day Doesn't Really Add Up to Much!

That's right. Keep buying three or four coffee drinks at Starbucks every day during the week. So what if it's $15 or $20 a day, every single day? What does that even amount to? Five to seven thousand dollars a year? Who cares?

Those few thousands here and there don't mean a damned thing, so don't even think about them at all. You're not some little mole burrowed in a cave pinching pennies. You're a free spirit, as I keep saying. If a couple of caffe mochas served up by a college-age cutie make the difference for you today . . . and tomorrow . . . and the next day . . . then go for it!

# 51

## $ $ $

### Find a Man or Woman with Really Expensive Tastes and Reckless Financial Habits— and Marry Him or Her!

One must avoid being lonely at all costs, so you need to have someone in your life at all times. And what better person to live with than someone who recklessly spends your money? These are the people who will buy fun things for themselves or for you (with your dough), who insist on taking lavish vacations, and who toss around $100 bills (yours) as if they were Pringles potato chips.

But don't just hang around with these kinds of people—marry one of them! Your mate (let's say it's a woman for the sake of example) will quickly find many new, fun ways to squander money—and again, what else is more fun? Maybe she'll find ways to gamble your money away (we haven't even gotten to that one yet!), charge extravagantly on your credit cards, "lose" money that you give her to buy groceries, and just somehow find a way to make your little domestic ship of financial well-being capsize.

Don't even think about marrying some cautious little squirrel who saves money and never spends any of it. Those people are dull, unsexy, dictatorial wet blankets. Instead of that, only associate with the fun people who like to spend, and see where that takes you. *Hint:* I guarantee it will keep you up at night.

# 52

## $ $ $

## Get Separated and Divorced Frequently

It doesn't really cost that much to get divorced. You just have to divide every single freakin' thing you own in half and give it away. But what do you care? You're not a scale. You're not a balance sheet. You're a soul who has to be happy no matter what the cost—and be damned with trying to work things out! It's better to lose half of what you own and have to pay alimony and child support—or receive those things and lose your house—than to tolerate even a second's worth of discomfort.

In fact, you should be *looking* for reasons to get divorced. There will always be plenty of them if you look hard enough. It stirs the pot to keep things moving in your life. It keeps you on your toes. You won't get complacent.

So what if a couple of divorce settlements can cripple even the most affluent man or woman? Your independence and self-respect are worth a heck of a lot more than mere money. And what about compromise and turning the other cheek? Well, maybe that's all right for losers and weaklings, but not for you. You demand your freedom and your dignity, and if you have to pay a lot for it, it's well worth that sordid money. You'll always make a lot more now that you're not tied down anyway.

And by the way, you're really going to be thrilled to see how reasonable divorce lawyers are. They hardly charge a dime. For the most part, they just want to help you out of a difficult patch in your life and don't care about money at all.

(And all of this doesn't even take into account how much fun it is to be alone—especially when you're wrinkled, saggy and middle-aged!)

# 53

## $ $ $

## Don't Keep Records

No record keeping for you! That's for librarians and bookkeepers and hermits. And anyway, since you're never going to have a financial plan and are never going to need money for retirement, why would you need to keep records?

Look at it this way. Suppose it's a nice, relaxing evening. You could spend it on the deck of your apartment drinking daiquiris, you could use the time to watch *Jimmy Kimmel Live* on TV, you could make some calls to your friends to tell them about the creepy date you had last night . . . or, you could spend your time filing statements from your bank or broker while standing next to some rusty old file cabinet.

Which sounds like more fun? And when that time comes when the IRS asks for your records for the last five years, just tell them that you're not a clerk and you don't have no wicked records, man! They'll understand.

Plus, if your broker makes a mistake and you don't have the records to prove she's wrong, so what? The IRS will just take your word for it. Just have another cocktail and another buffalo chicken wing and soon you won't even remember that it's almost tax time—oh, but that's right, you don't pay taxes.

Ah, life is good!

# 54

## $ $ $

## Gamble with Your Money

This may seem a bit obvious, but let me explain. It seems that a lot of otherwise decent folks are just scared to gamble with their money. This is silly. It's a great deal of fun to visit a casino or a racetrack and plunk down your dough . . . and then let Lady Luck have her way with you.

Casinos and racetracks are fascinating places. There are lots of good-looking men and women, as well as food stands and restaurants and bars to eat and drink in—basically, a good time just waiting to happen. And there's also the chance—in your case, a certainty—of making a heap o' cash. The roulette wheel, if you play it right, pays off something like 36 to one. Those are much better odds than working for 40 years!

And the racetrack? Have you ever heard of a prefecta? A trifecta? Do you have any clue how much they can pay off? It can be stupendous. Thousands to one. You can go in with a $5 ticket and walk out with enough money to buy a house . . . if you were foolish enough to buy a house.

Why forego that pleasure? Why not gamble your money on the possibility that your life could suddenly change on a dime (or a two-dollar ticket!) or a card in a blackjack hand or even seven numbers in a lottery? Why not give yourself a shot at doing something truly magnificent with only a few dollars down?

And let's not forget sports betting. It's thrilling! You know what I mean—that adrenaline rush you get when you realize that if your team doesn't make a touchdown you'll lose $10,000! But if you do win . . . wow, you could be set for a long time! So why not make bets on as many games as you can? What could possibly be more rewarding than spending a Sunday watching three TVs with a different football game on each, knowing that you have money riding on every one of them? I mean, when you think about it, it's really no fun at all to just watch a game without betting on it— that's for losers! And when you win big and the bookie sends over your money, hey, champ, that's when things really start to sizzle!

So, go for it, pal, live it up, and have fun, fun, fun—and also know in your heart that you're really helping people out, too. You're probably aware that gambling is one of the few rapidly growing businesses in this country—heck, Native American tribes depend on it for their livelihood! And there wouldn't be any gleaming palaces in Las Vegas without gambling. Atlantic City, in fact, would still be a pitiful backwater without it.

So have yourself a great time and know that you're helping Native American children get scholarships; that you're contributing to the construction of gorgeous buildings in the desert; that you're providing employment for card dealers, showgirls, and hookers . . . and that you're lighting the candle that shoots you to the moon, baby, to the moon!

# 55

## $ $ $

## Don't Bother to Provide for Your Spouse or Your Children

Why should you do anything for posterity? What the heck has posterity ever done for you? Aren't your kids always asking for things? Aren't they a pain in the neck? Why should you feel that you owe them a thing? Wouldn't they be better off anyway if they had to work for everything they got, like Abe Lincoln or Andrew Carnegie?

Don't bother sacrificing one single thing for your kids or your spouse so that they'll be better off or well provided for when you die. What will it mean to you? You'll be dead anyway. Why should you have to sacrifice a trip or a new boat to buy insurance for your family? It's all about you, you, you, anyway, and once you're gone, the world ends, too. What possible concern could it be of yours that your spouse or kids might have to scrimp and save when you're gone? They're only your flesh and blood.

What about setting up accounts for your kids so they can pay for college or make a down payment on a home? No way. There are scholarships. There are student loans and jobs. Or they can go without college. It might do them good to go out and work right after high school. Why coddle them with money when you could have so much more fun coddling yourself?

So basically, just devote your life to thinking about your own wants and needs, and let the chips fall where they may.

*But you knew all this already, didn't you? You're a real winner—through and through!*

# AFTERWORD

## $ $ $

Well, all righty then. If you've read this far, it's just possible that you have some idea what you're doing wrong. It just may be the case that you've noticed you're doing a lot of the aforementioned ruinous things that spell T-R-O-U-B-L-E in your financial life. It could be that you're not saving regularly. Perhaps you're supporting three households due to your frequent divorces. Maybe you plunk down money on stocks based on overheard tips and rumors. Most likely, you simply have no plan whatsoever and prefer not to think about your finances at all.

Well, let me assure you that if you just keep on doing what you're doing, things will only get worse. I've said it before in this book and I'll say it again: "If nothing changes, nothing changes." If you keep doing even a few of the 55 things I've mentioned, you're going to wind up in drastic circumstances down the road—or you'll remain there if that's your situation now.

But if you just start doing a few of the following, you might be amazed at the difference it makes in your life:

- Save as much as you can on a regular basis.

- Invest conservatively—for example, in very broad stock-market indexes, variable annuities, and short-term broad-based mutual funds, Treasury or high-grade corporate bonds.

- Buy your own home, buy your own home, buy your own home, buy your own home, buy your own home.

- Avoid doing business with people unless they have a good reputation for probity and integrity, and if you can't find out anything about them, don't let them anywhere near your money!

- Remember that spending is not a substitute for saving.

- Remind yourself continually that life goes by with stunning, breath-taking speed, and you will want to prepare for the day when you no

longer have the strength to work—
or at least to work as hard as you
did when you were young—and
such preparation primarily takes
the form of saving.

- Leave fancy gimmicks to stupid
  people.

- Know that there are no free lunches
  anywhere once your parents die,
  that you are the primary person responsible for you, and that caring
  for your family is a moral duty—
  and this includes being careful with
  your money.

Or, to boil it all down to an even denser
soup, here are two final pieces of advice: The first
one is from my father and he said it to me with
love—and just the fact that he thought I would
understand it was a high tribute. "Benjy," he
said, "live prudently."

I don't do it often enough, but I do it occasionally.

The other remark, even simpler, is from
Bernard Baruch, that Wise Man of money who
advised Presidents on financial matters for 40

years. After World War I, he was asked what advice he had for Americans in the new postwar world. He replied simply, "Work and save."

$ $ $

# ACKNOWLEDGMENTS

## $ $ $

This book was made possible by the generosity and confidence of Louise Hay, Reid Tracy, and Jill Kramer at Hay House; by the kind support of my wife and my dear pals Barron Thomas, Steve Gage, and Sid Dauman; and by the constant companionship of my wonderful angelic dog, Brigid.

The primary inspirations for the rules came from my father, Herbert Stein; my mother, Mildred Stein; and my sister, Rachel Epstein. I also learned a great deal from my former agent, a superbly smart investor named George Diskant; from the fabulous Hathaway family (father Frank and daughter Karen) who run the best-managed real-estate company in America, and who are both super-smart people with 100 percent integrity; and by Al Burton, genius producer.

I was, and still am, privileged to have been taught by the great Milton Friedman, the greatest economist since Adam Smith and a dear family friend; by Professor C. Lowell Harriss, also a great scholar of economics; by the legendary James Tobin of Yale and his colleague, Henry Wallich; by Larry Lissitzyn—by trade a lawyer but profoundly wise about money; by the immortal Warren Buffett, whose maxims about money and investing are priceless; by my long-time, highly capable broker, Kevin Hanley; and by Alan Abelson and Jim Meagher of *Barron's*.

The largest contribution by far came from the great suggestions of my frequent co-author, one of the smartest, quickest, and most mentally well-organized persons I've ever met, my dear friend Phil DeMuth. His help made writing this book a breeze. If it is of any value, he gets most of the credit. If it is useless, the fault is all mine.

# ABOUT THE AUTHOR

$ $ $

**Ben Stein** was born in Washington, D.C., and grew up in Silver Spring, Maryland. He studied economics at Columbia University and was also lucky enough to study finance at Yale while he attended Yale Law School. Ben has served as an economist, trial lawyer, speech-writer, teacher of law and economics, columnist for *The Wall Street Journal,* writer on finance (especially financial fraud), for *Barron's,* commentator on finance on television, frequent witness at Congressional hearings about finance, and author of many books about personal finance (none as funny as this one).

Ben has been well known in Hollywood for his roles in many movies, most notably *Ferris Bueller's Day Off;* for his continuing roles in *The Wonder Years* and *Charles in Charge;* and for his long-running game show, *Win Ben Stein's Money.*

Ben lives in Southern California with his wife, son, and many beloved dogs and cats.

# $$$ Notes $$$

# $$$ Notes $$$

# $$$ Notes $$$

# $$$ Notes $$$

We hope you enjoyed this Hay House book.
If you would like to receive a free catalog featuring additional
Hay House books and products, or if you would like
information about the Hay Foundation, please contact:

Hay House, Inc.
P.O. Box 5100
Carlsbad, CA 92018-5100

**(760) 431-7695** or **(800) 654-5126**
**(760) 431-6948 (fax)** or **(800) 650-5115 (fax)**
**www.hayhouse.com**

$ $ $

*Published and distributed in Australia by:*
Hay House Australia, Ltd. • 18/36 Ralph St. • Alexandria NSW
2015 • *Phone:* 612-9669-4299 • *Fax:* 612-9669-4144 •
www.hayhouse.com.au

*Published and distributed in the United Kingdom by:*
Hay House UK, Ltd. • Unit 62, Canalot Studios •
222 Kensal Rd., London W10 5BN • *Phone:* 44-20-8962-1230 •
*Fax:* 44-020-8962-1239 • www.hayhouse.co.uk

*Published and distributed*
*in the Republic of South Africa by:*
Hay House SA (Pty), Ltd., P.O. Box 990, Witkoppen 2068 •
*Phone/Fax:* 2711-7012233 • orders@psdprom.co.za

*Distributed in Canada by:*
Raincoast • 9050 Shaughnessy St., Vancouver, B.C. V6P 6E5 •
*Phone:* (604) 323-7100 • *Fax:* (604) 323-2600

$ $ $

Sign up via the Hay House USA Website to receive the
Hay House online newsletter and stay informed about what's
going on with your favorite authors. You'll receive bimonthly
announcements about: Discounts and Offers, Special Events,
Product Highlights, Free Excerpts, Giveaways, and more!